"A wonderful, sometimes eth
reaches of all our minds. Ver
Highly recommended."
*- Shaun Hutson (Iconic horror writer and author of Slugs, Breeding
Ground, Spawn, Testament)*

"He's taken the candle of his imagination into some
dark places and from them has pulled poetry... There
are many truths here."
*- Nicholas Vince (Chatterer in Hellraiser, Writer of What Monsters
Do and Other People's Darkness)*

"Every poem pulses with raw feeling. A hauntingly
evocative and strikingly personal collection of
remarkable poetry from a name we are destined to one
day find very familiar."
*- Kealan Patrick Burke (Bram Stoker Award-Winning author of Kin
and Sour Candy)*

"Quite the debut. This is a book you definitely what to
check out, to see exactly what poetry can be."
*- Liian Varus (Poet and author of Oh, To Be Human and Is
Stranged)*

"A daring volume which delves into the darkest corners
of the human mind... packs one heck of a punch. "
- David Gelmini (Dread Central)

"...Brutally truthful and abrasively hopeful. A very brave
and vulnerable book."
- J.M. Ritch (Poet and author of The Heart is a Tree Cut Down)

"Poetry and horror fans alike will be drawn to the beauty, darkness and brutal honesty in this, N.P.Hunt's debut book. "

- Ria Fend (Designer, Actor and Screenwriter)

To Shawn,

thank you so much for taking
the time to read my work and
for contributing your kind words.
I really appreciate it.
All the best

IMMORTALISED IN INK
A BOOK OF POETRY
BY N.P. HUNT

NP Hunt

Edited by Vincent Heselwood, Martin Redmond, Ria Fend
Cover design by Ria Fend
Design, layout and production management by Ria Fend

Illustrated by Andy Hosegood (pg 17, 31, 75, 81 and 117)
and Coral Davies @tattooed.reef.artworks (pg 22, 53 and 59)

ISBN: 9781838235208 (paperback)
ISBN: 9781838235215 (ebook)

Dedicated to my Mum,
who always encouraged
me to write.

FOREWORD

Firstly, thank you for reading this. It means the world to me that anyone would take the time to read my work and I hope there is something in these pages to make it a good experience for you. For a long time, the idea of putting any of my writing out into the world was a terrifying prospect, but finally getting started in my writing career was the best move I ever made.

Being fairly inept at human relationships, I'm extremely lucky to have a select few people in my life who have supported and encouraged me. Without those people I certainly would never have had the courage to release a collection like this one. But thanks and appreciation are for the acknowledgements section. I'm not entirely convinced that many people, except myself, ever read forewords and introductions, but I figured some background and context might be interesting to some.

I have been writing poetry for around twenty three years, and some of the work I've included dates all the way back to when I started 'dabbling' back in high school. Hefty edits and rewrites were needed over the years (as well as the vast majority being outright deleted), but in one or two cases the bones of the work were actually not terrible. Nothing from that time has survived in its entirety, but there are a couple that have evolved from some of those early attempts.

My earlier writing was influenced as much by lyricists as traditional poets, and although I have a lot of literary influences, I still rank some of the poetry from the likes of

Roddy Woomble, Michael Stipe, Hope Sandoval and Jason Lytle (amongst many others) as being up there with the likes of Poe, Tennyson, Blake, Byron and Hardy et al. Whether set to music or making its own, poetry is poetry.

Although the obvious Poe, Hardy and Blake influences are probably the most evident in my work, I get inspiration from everywhere and in a variety of ways, including from visual artists like Shawn Coss, John Bramblitt, and Socorro Martinez, and contemporary writers like Sarah Kay, Max Porter, Brenna Twohy, Liian Varus, Emily Berry and Ken Arkind.

I essentially gave up on writing for a few years, although it was never a conscious decision. Mental health issues and other unpleasant factors took over and I drifted away from it, as with many other interests and passions. But, after I was encouraged by my friend, Vincent, to start writing articles for a website, I gained the confidence to expand and share some of my other writing. I had randomly put out a few poems and short stories and despite encouraging feedback, I filed everything away and got busy with other projects. I kept adding new poems here and there, but constantly got distracted by the next exciting project or idea, so there was never a specific goal for my poetry beyond the enjoyment and catharsis of writing it. I thought I might put out a collection one day, but had no idea in what form or how.

Every now and then, I would get an idea for a poem or a line that I just had to get out, and invariably the idea soon spilled over into a first draft. Before long I realised that I had built up a fairly substantial collection.

I wanted to do something with all of this work, and the obvious route would be to publish it, but as my own harshest critic (like many other creative people), I found ways to talk myself out of it and reasons to procrastinate. It was all just a vague idea, but when I was seeing a counsellor for depression-related issues, he encouraged me to look into publishing my work and to be generally more active in pursuing my ambitions as a writer. This also coincided with being made redundant from my day-job as a security guard, which gave me an additional push in the right direction.

I started putting everything together - overhauling my collection whilst serving my notice and simultaneously starting work for a new company. While that was going on, the Covid-19 coronavirus pandemic was reaching the UK, creating even more uncertainty for the future. With some deep frown lines and an air laced with profanities, I was eventually able to finalise this collection whilst also working on my new collected crime article website and my author profile website.

If one thing stands out about my creative writing, it is probably that the vast majority is quite dark. Some of that stems from the works that inspire and motivate me, as I definitely tend to prefer poetry and fiction with dark themes and explore the bleaker side of human experience and emotion. Some of it also stems from my experience with depression, which has been a major inspiration behind a lot of my work.

I have always felt that mental health and promoting mental wellbeing is incredibly important, and open discussion about all aspects of mental illness is vital.

Mental health issues have affected many people in my life and I strongly believe that it is something which desperately needs more awareness, research and accessible treatment for anyone who may be suffering. I believe sharing our emotions and experiences, even the unpleasant ones (and sometimes, especially the unpleasant ones), can not only be therapeutic for the person expressing them, but for anyone who receives that message and relates to it in some way.

We can sometimes find surprising comfort in knowing that someone else is down there with us, or that they have been where we are and have managed to move past it, especially if they feel like there is no hope and no escape. If anyone reading this is feeling that way right now, I want you to know that there is something better coming for you soon. You may not believe it or be able to see it, but someday it will come. Please reach out to friends and family or contact your doctor or The Samaritans for help. You can also find several groups on social media where communities offer each other support. Please don't be silent. Tell someone.

As well as the darker subjects and emotions, there are also poems in here about love, life, hope and overcoming obstacles, tributes to inspirational figures and homages to classic literature. Hopefully it will include at least one thing you value and/or enjoy.

Whether you picked up this book for distraction, entertainment, reassurance or kinship, I genuinely hope that you find what you are looking for.

~ N.P. Hunt.

CONTENTS

IMMORTALISED IN INK

SONGS OF REBELLION

LOVE AND EARNED SELF-LOATHING

OF KNOWING OTHER PEOPLE

THE EVIL OF THE MIND

FRIENDS ARE CRUEL ENDINGS

REACHING EVER UPWARDS

IMMORTALISED IN INK

"Art is the lie that enables us to realize the truth."

- Pablo Picasso

IN INFINITUM OBSCURA

Little black book full of questions,
what's your story?
Keep secrets for the one who loved you
once upon a time.
Take time out to share with us your wisdom,
little lost book,
So mistakes are not repeated
and we rectify forgotten crime.
Cramped scribbles and prose
tells a story of a wise man,
But where was his mind
when he left you here for us to find?
Are we all prone to wisdom
or was he special, little torn book?
Do you even have the answers,
or were they also left behind?
Did he love or tolerate you?
A blessing, curse or gift bestowed?
Answers kept selfishly in secret,
without disclosing hints or clues,
Filled with enigmas between your covers
and spillages of thought,
I create new endings for his stories
and yet they still remain as true.
Observations, fabrications
and sets of rules to follow to nowhere.
'Reveal the answers that I seek,
or I'll liberate your truths in fire!'
Deceptions of imagination
or flights of innocent pretence?

Are these ramblings eternal truths,
or the golden spinnings of a liar?
Wise men without faces
write unashamed and unchallenged.
I may be crazy or pretending,
with this book I've never owned.
Marked 'In Infinitum Obscura'
in sunken letters on your skin,
Found by chance when wandering;
my destination still unknown.
With truths and lies I add my own tales,
building mountains out of dirt.
Blank spaces closing inwards now,
in swirls of honest ink and flora,
I remove my face to fit alongside,
though exposed, ashamed and alert.
'A fool masquerading as a wise man
seeks to stay In Infinitum Obscura.'
Meaning less of masks than rejecting ideas
of the beyond now and forever,
It would indeed be Infinitely Dark
had the title been '*Ad* Infinitum Obscura'.
Yet still in title and in deed,
through the passing on of what time has severed,
I'm left unsettled in the knowledge
that my best additions are all much poorer.
Heads buried in sands of home comforts
and hoping to fade away,
Disappearing over horizons
without the integrity or aim of an explorer.

Hearing echoes of folktales on breezes,
as the elders gather and say
'You are doomed to your fate if you are tempted to stay
In Infinitum Obscura.'
Even this creative license,
which I entrusted to myself alone,
Fell short of mythos deemed worthy
of my palette of privileged tastes,
So I welcome the blindfold
to block the progress of time's own,
While I add scribbles to a masterpiece
to save fortune from waste.

DALI AND THE ELEPHANTS

Expressive is, as attention does,
Both bright and dark in Eastern clothes,
Elephants march on fragile limbs
While fluid time consumes all things.

Freudian slip into something complex,
Inheritance lost without any context,
No praise too faint, surrounded by sycophants,
Yet still deserved for Persistence and elephants.

In physical space and creating illusions,
Surreal and stark in religious confusion,
Find order in chaos and uplift the disastrous,
Build a village on water and a living on canvas.

Multiple Christs suspended in space,
Hide their agony by turning their face.
Tigers leap when bees disturb sleep,
Obsession with death is not a secret you keep.

Disembodied dreams and unnatural placements;
Labelled a conspirator towards art's debasement.
Yet narcissus transforms to survive cast in stone,
Reputation preserved on your merit alone.

TUMBLING

Tumbling down before me
Coloured so with jealousy,
The most beautiful thing I have ever seen
That never spoke or moved or breathed.
And people speeding by there
That did not see me there,
All on the way to the place where
They can remain blissfully unaware,
Ignore my wondering penchant
For destruction of beautiful things,
By twisting nature's nature
To see what inspiration it can bring.

WARHOL

Andy lived a shared dream yesterday,
With community spirit
in an alternative way,
Rejects-are-us
and in the name of our art,
We'll reject vague traditions
to make a new start.

Bohemian ideals
of a life without order;
Mass-produced contrast
to counteract borders.
Art be the power
and music sells the glory,
Icons of the zeitgeist
become the whole story.

A rose-tinted life
with Velvet Underground dreams
Stripped down restrictions
to reject how things seem.
Hedonistic heroics
and fanatical fandom
Made stars of outcasts
and shone light on the random.

Living behind disguises
    and offering cans of soup,
        He built a factory of dreams
            for the world as one group.
        An examination of capitalism,
    ironically, lead to gains,
Exploding Plastic Inevitable
    unites the arts in one refrain.

        Survivor of bullets and circumstance,
    and of scrutiny and slander,
        Refusing to conform
            or to compromise
        or pander.
Shattering the norms
        and exceeding all the limits,
            Andy predicted the starstruck
    would get their own 15 minutes.

Collecting and hoarding the intriguing and strange,
    Capturing moments
        among attempts to rearrange.
On the lips of the masses,
    yet still on the brink,
        Immortalised in legend
        and on film
            and in ink.

DRAWING THE SKY

When I was a child,
I liked to draw the sky in chalk.
Blue skies, cloudy skies,
night skies and stormy skies.
It was a living kaleidoscope,
showcasing multitudes of moveability
and unpredictable change.
The beautiful shades of darkening blues,
dusky purples, and the pinks of the dawn
were vibrant and powerful,
and there was no such thing as wrong
in the arrangement of clouds
or the placement of the sun or the moon.
The land beneath was always secondary,
because the sky was everything.
But when I didn't have the right colours,
I would just draw something else.
There could be no sky without the pinks,
blues or purples to breathe it to life.

When you were a child,
I know you liked to draw the sky too.
Your sky would always be peaceful,
because to you it was a calm sea,
which hung silently
behind whatever noise
was going on closer to earth.
The colours could be anything and everything,
even if all you had to draw with was charcoal.
It didn't matter to you
if the colours were correct or not.
You believed the sky was beautiful,
even in the blacks and greys
of the charcoal on concrete flags.
Even your monochrome rainbows
looked better than the real thing,
and your sky was always alive with birds
whose song could almost be heard
from within the stillness.

It was a sky we shared,
and we both saw its beauty
in different ways.
But it moved us each to capture it,
just as it had captured us.
And those drawings of the sky
told us so much more than
how the clouds had looked that day.

A LETTER TO THE INTERNAL EDITOR

Dear Internal Editor,

I'd thank you for your input if it wasn't so destructive.

You lurk over my mind's shoulder with constant, faceless criticisms, but what have you created yourself? All you ever do is destroy and malign. You show me every weakness in my art, and you take pride in your artless approach.

Your pen is always poised to obliterate, rarely allowing a single waking thought to linger and find its own life.

How many turns of phrase have you turned into doubt?

How many times have your cruel judgements and harsh, wicked tones been the soundtrack to just giving up?

You should feel ashamed for the shame you've cast upon me. and I'm not the only one.

A million of you and a million of us, the faithful vessels awaiting their muses, only for you to scoff and sneer when they strike. Each to their own, with their own insults and ways to get under our skins.

But this is not about the rest.

This is about you and me, because you made this business personal.

Your questioning eye seems uncomfortable. Is critique of your critique hurting your feelings? Do you fear that it reflects on all of your abilities and all of the work that came before this moment? Are you experiencing what you make us feel each and every day?

At least allow me the courtesy to finish before you start ripping my words from the page. A small amount of restraint might make it far less crippling.

You have killed so many.

Don't get me wrong, I know that you have value, but you also have your place. Creation is no time for pragmatism. The science of the thing comes later.

First, allow the thing to flow and grow and become. It needs the room to breathe before we go back together and shape it into something more beautiful. We can hack away the ugly parts and fix the details of it all another day.

But it has to be born first.

So I hope we have an understanding, but I suspect I'll be hearing from you soon. I know that you mean well. Most of the time.

Please be kind.
Or be gentle.

Forever yours and kind regards, or some such perfunctory nicety...

From your eternal servant,

The Writer

PLEASE DISTURB

Please disturb me for artistic delight;
As revelling in pain can reveal hidden light.
I'll cast you in sunbeams so you'll live on forever
If you bring me discomfort to feed my endeavours.

In disturbance, finding peace in catharsis,
The joy of pain, making adults from artists.
Hence my request to disturb me at length,
Become one of those in whom others find strength.

Read me; I'm open, with an interesting title.
View me; on show, though not naked, not frightful.
Exposed and delighted to be here today,
Telling of things that the target can't say.

Disturbed, yet still focused and madly involved,
Making up mysteries for our other lies to solve,
Saving falsehoods and lives at the stroke of a key,
Living other paths and eras - though static, set free.

Life gets in the way and yet informs inspiration,
Experiences borrowed, shared through imagination.
Celebrate our trials, for through fires we ignite
Disturbances for the benefit of artistic delight.

THE BALLAD OF MARK ANTONY

Let Rome in Tiber melt before me,
And for you I'll go to war at sea.
You are my queen of Egyptian fame
But let not this end in tragedy.
If I am grey, let me be Anthony,
For blinded am I (by love for thee)
Yet, I am more with you than ever before;
But a shadow of the shell that you set free.

Sacrifice myself for you, my Queen,
Then may you sacrifice yourself for me?
Nothing dramatic is becoming of me,
For I am grey and not really free.

Contradict my own beliefs again,
Less to impress, but with blood of more men.
Mere man am I and not to be blamed,
The son of the betrayed, betrayed by me again.
Brutus, my friend, has rubbed off on me
Though motives may differ, that's plain to see.
I am consumed in this lustful fantasy
Which is not becoming of a grey man like me.

So let Rome in Tiber melt before me
As for you I set sail for war at sea.
I love you, my Queen of Egyptian fame
So ignore warnings of my growing insanity.
Our brotherhood ceased by the son of the betrayed,
So pray as I might to win war at sea,
Against my emperor, brother, general, friend
I feel the impending doom of our tragedy.

THE INSTINCT DEFENCE

Lurking in the shadows slyly,
in the recesses of time.
Hidden from mortal vision
and safely masking every sign
Of what I have become,
despite my decadence sublime.
Craving darkness, passion
and transubstantiated wine.

Everlasting lifeline costs me less
than Faustus or Mr. Gray.
And in the course of nature,
when there is still some price to pay,
Instinct to survive and strength
dictates who becomes our prey.
Costing me nothing but hope and light
(and guilt for what I attained).

Stranger of God - but with power enough -
to be a threat and to compete,
A gentleman with grace and substance,
but with a divinely evil streak.
If 'evil' is what you call it...
but it's just instinct if you ask me.
Fear be my tool and in faith and in wood,
you may yet find my defeat.

Spawned from myths and legends,
in sullied afterbirth of Abraham,
Embracing long lost symbols,
clothed in candlelight and pentagrams.
The names I've been given (cast asunder in spite),
by people just like you,
Include devil, demon, monster, fiend;
and once again I stand accused.

But just as lions are not evil
when they prey on antelope,
Neither am I when I hunt my own kind,
or erase your tortured hope.
So the instinct defence will serve me well
as I write upon these pages.
It consoles me for days, asleep in my grave,
living on throughout the ages.

VICTOR'S ABOMINATION

Born of curiosity
and of arrogance and of sin,
Called abomination;
oversized, in failing skin.
I have done the world no wrong
and I had never asked to live,
Yet the blame is all on me
for the unwanted gifts you give.

Only safe in hiding,
seeking refuge from the cold, harsh frost,
Finding kinship in the worn-out pages
of Milton's Paradise Lost,
Longing for some purpose
and just wanting to belong,
Mistaken for a monster,
without the power to be strong.

This Prometheus of modern times,
but without the dedication,
Brought me into being
but was ashamed of his creation,
Abandoned me in fear,
for he is both genius and a liar,
Inflicting life in spite of God,
but denied the gift of fire.

If you leave me cold and lonely,
without family or faction,
I'll rob you of your brethren
and come to blackmail you to action.
Tragedy becomes us,
because we came from tragic starts,
From loss and grief and longing,
from unions torn apart.

We both are bound by oaths of blood
to fight against all takers,
Because each of us is driven by
the loss of our own makers.
We will hunt each other down
to seek redemption for the past,
Until defeating death and nature
has destroyed us both at last.

ROLL UP

Roll up another storytime,
      then off to fields of dreams;
           Vibrant shades and colours;
    in parts community and creed.
          So we'll have another measure
    and conversations surely flow,
Numbness blocks out badness,
      so the happiness can glow and grow.

         Black sheep of your genus,
    with relief and beauty rendered,
Correlation and causation,
      confused to serve agendas,
         Yet prohibition fails
            and stories spread to every quarter,
         At storytime we roll our own
    and restore our world to order.

Nourished by your nature
      and savouring your taste,
         Benefitting mind and soul,
            not a second spent in waste.
         Roll up in newfound friendship
    and with those we've always known,
Roll up another storytime,
      and we'll tell stories of our own.

SONGS OF REBELLION

"Usually when people are sad, they don't do anything. They just cry over their condition. But when they get angry, they bring about a change."

- Malcolm X

THE LEGACY OF BATTLE

Choose your weapon well,
as it's the last thing you'll ever hold,
It will be the subject of your final chapter,
unless your legend remains untold.
Create your myth in sections,
with each selection carefully made,
Tales are rooted in details
and they dictate which memories fade.

Select your armour wisely
And bear a banner of which you're proud,
Comrades and songs will be chosen for you,
But hold them close and sing them loud.

Blinded by the endgame
and serving crusades which seem unjust,
Finding solace in appointed enemies'
assumed evil and unholy lusts.
Each dragon slain in envy
adds to your arsenal and your vaults,
But covetous eyes and usurpers
are drawn by your own fault.

BOUND APART

Bound apart by political silence
Hiding our heritage in blindfolded tongue
Expressions squashed in aesthetic decline
Splintered and shattered by plastic denial

Fractured trains of dying thought
Breed bad decisions of enforced divisions
Parades for poverty without a hint of irony
Less for the pride than for other forms of credit

Essential decadence, blatantly obscured
Guarded communion in group isolation
Failure to win, with no stake for the taking
Brilliance in idiocy and hope in the dark

Technology saves us from our primitive selves
Acting out scenes where we were not torn apart
Ancient unions are revived by our present
The scabs of blood-oaths washed in saltwater unity

Rudeness dressed as honour; insults build self-esteem
Flushing our riches and collecting cheap trinkets
Hiding the grace of years behind false ignorance
We are gagged by our arrogance, in chains of loose string

COVID-19
(THE FIRST DAYS)

New threat from nature, death comes unseen,
Fear found a new name in Covid-19.
Cruel hands are creeping, the panic obscene,
Selfishly hoarding before quarantine.
Take natural steps, such as keeping hands clean,
Keeping our distance, yet the selfish convene.
Beginnings of lockdown, the ignorant seen
Flaunting cruel disregard for those without means.
The weak are dispensable, or so it would seem,
Pray you're not vulnerable, with nowhere to lean.
Still learning to fight it, without hope for vaccine,
As the fear still grows stronger of Covid-19.
The lowliest workers all have to stick to routine,
Denied the same protections as their management teams.
Minimum wage lab rats to act as a screen,
Keeping up the illusion that the world lost no steam.
No cure and no care, no help intervenes,
Not yet understood, this vicious Covid-19.

And this danger comes soon, for you and for me,
Fear knows no riches, measured only in screams.
And it comes for us all, whether mild or extreme,
The whole world will bear scars from cruel Covid-19.
But we find good in humans, which we all rarely see,
Beginning on balconies, the trapped set themselves free,
To entertain and to share, without any scheme,
Building bridges to people,
while keeping space in between.
Then there are the heroes for the health war-machine,
Battling in scrubs to keep us swimming upstream,
Risking their lives where most wouldn't dream,
Keeping the world turning despite Covid-19.
No thanks for the many, but that was foreseen,
Not done for the credit, just in hope for reprieve.
We shall fight on in defiance, our hope evergreen,
For the world shall not crumble under Covid-19.

FAITHLESS

Believe me if you're weak in mind,
I will not ever comfort you.
Too weak to seek what you cannot find,
Logic often usurps truth.
Why find that which is not lost,
Or fix things which are not broken?
Laughter is wasted and at what cost?
Yet I offer you no token.
Talk of forgiveness is less than cheap
And cheap talk is a human machine.
Hypocrites speak of truth and yet leap
Into notions and actions which truth finds obscene.

WANDERING AND WONDERING

Destruction is looming
      around every twisting turn,
            Indiscriminately stealing,
      forcing ownership to burn,
Transfixed eyes forced to watch,
      but seldom do they learn,
            We're left wandering and wondering,
            unable to discern.

Existence fleeting rapidly
      and all around will soon adjourn,
            Falling from grace like the first of us,
              sentenced never to return.
            A stoic gait hides the shame
      of your fears and of your concerns,
Victory eclipses weakness,
      as you claim what you have earned.

ANTHEM FOR DISILLUSIONED YOUTH

This world is crumbling into ethical dust
So we sing and we speak of the things that we must.
Loud and with force to make sure that we're heard
Step into the spotlight to speak the right words.
You can break all the rules that they can set
And accrue all the material things we can get,
But they rape, pillage and manipulate the nation
So action is the mouthpiece for our generation.

We are just children, full of frustration:
Longing for the heart and soul of innovation
To move us in ways that tell us our own story
Or fill us with hope, or with luck, or with glory.
Sing songs of rebellion and sadness and truth,
Empowered by anthems for disillusioned youth.

With no damage done and skin still intact,
Not due to a legend, but based solely on facts.
This pain makes no difference and to hurt is to fall,
People instigate hatred and we must answer the call.
Take the fight to the people and the leaders fear eruptions
As we take to the streets to confront all corruption.
We will burn down our cities and never retreat,
Forgiveness is weakness and we shall not taste defeat.

The change in the air, left unbreathed, has turned stale
So we suffocate the enemies who willed us to fail.
They denied us our voices when we wished to be heard,
And now they are deafened by the rage they incurred.
Now we are counted and we will fight to stay true
To uplift our vulnerable and rebuild the world anew
We shall seek balanced justice; eye for eye, tooth for tooth,
Progress will be earned and won by disillusioned youth.

FROM THE DARK SIDE OF MAN

Glint of light receding, retreating out of fear,
Loss of human feeling, decreasing by the year,
Hatred is still growing as we indulge the shed of tears,
The fall of brothers welcomed
as our horizons draw still near.

Memories tainted and fast fading, lost in history's arrears,
Consumed by making misery into lifestyles and careers,
Swallowed by the selfish and all that they hold dear,
Protests from the human hearts
have fallen on deaf ears.

Now that we're voiceless, our ideas and thoughts banned,
We are defenceless to the masses,
bound by tongue and by hand.
Lulled into believing that we can't when we can,
The only true plans are from the dark side of man.

TO MY ALMIGHTY

A letter to my almighty, paper yellowed, ink now faded,
Catches in a breeze in a forgotten, lonely shrine.
Another prayer unanswered, another reason to feel jaded,
Playing saviour to a cause that I know was never mine.

Still, I am stunned that you took my innocence from me,
So now I have sacrificed my commitment from youth.
You have stolen and lost me and now I can't unsee,
I lost myself to you in the virus of your truth.

I eliminated you, but in an unended state
You stole from me, so I am on constant alert.
I spit at you and I raise a gesture of hate:
You are my nemesis, usurper and the cause of my hurt.

The world has wronged me in abundance
and I still feel unclean,
So now live through my loss; let my will inflict the same.
Crying in the night at your wrongs that have stained me,
You created my pain in the sake of your name.

BORN IN WHISPERS

Born in whispers, ending in screams,
With nothing but silence to fill in-between.
Ideas and desires in cold, abstract form
Are not fuel enough to keep the underflow warm.

Movement to action through learned obligation;
Necessary evil to promote fear and segregation.
Collateral damage and swelling arsenals of ballistics,
Bring about reflection under pressure from statistics.

Lost in the clouds beneath the apathetic water,
Stirring up the lakebed with blood and fire and mortar.
Division breeds false unity in campaigns lacking morals,
Support for wars and massacres
in support of rich men's quarrels.

Born into bloodshed and ending in fate,
With nothing but violence to alter our states.
Ideals are relics that we gave up for desires
To serve self-interested masters and torturous liars.

FRUSTRATION GENERATIONS

I need this, so leave me be.
This borrowed world is far from free
A carer to us, who we swore we created.
Swaddled in lies, passed around and castrated.

Pleased with ourselves at what we destroyed,
We turn on each other and pretend we're annoyed.
Who is the parent, and who is to blame?
Believe me, I beg you. They're hardly the same.

The kinds who have preyed on our cultures and nations
Will slowly tear down our rented accomodation,
So gather generations, full of frustration,
To cast off the damnation of past domination.

Your past is what makes you the you of today,
But the future is played on a much better stage,
So lay down preparations for taking a stand,
Frustration generations shall reclaim the land.

FALLING AT THE ALTAR

Falling at the altar
of a thousand dead ideals,
I pledged myself to burden,
in servitude to steal,
Handing over takings
from the poor and unsuspecting
To overlords who hurt us
and the ones we've been protecting.

My cloak and dagger methods
always earned the highest praise,
And I became the king of thieves,
but still remained a slave.
A vagabond with masters
who snatched up all my takings
To feed their greed with riches
and with aches of my own making.

I was bowing to dictators
and ignoring all distractions,
For I was taught that our beliefs
will always save us over actions.
Then I faltered at the dawning
of a new translucent sky,
As knowledge bred rejection
of indoctrinated lies.

It was hard to walk that road
with broken chains between my feet,
Not quite tied together,
but still weighed down by past defeats.
But I knew to stay determined,
so I clawed towards redemption,
Overcoming hurt
by giving hope my full attention.

We have cast aside our chains
and raised up triumphant sounds
For the old ideals have fallen
and now hope is all around.
And we believe no lies because of
the knowledge we have found,
So we shall fall no further,
as nothing casts us to the ground.

Freedom followed waking,
and now I wake myself much faster,
Unbound and standing proud
that I shall call no man my master.
Keys to unlock freedom
are revealed as hope increases,
The dictators have all fallen,
and their altar lies in pieces.

THE LORD OF EVERYTHING

Watch a dream die before your eyes,
And feel it inside and try not to cry.
Then you may strive to ask yourself why
We're all just so desperate to just stay alive?

I am the potter and you are my clay,
There's no excuse left and nothing to say.
I am the master and I am the king,
I am the lord of everything.

In the moon's spotlight, I stand by my plans,
As I prepare to take flight and conquer your lands.
Your dreams will collapse like time's cruelest sands,
As I gather my harvest with crooked, cold hands.

Any strength is illusion and the power is mine,
I shall rule over you until the end of all time.
I am the master and I am the king
I am the lord of everything.

Watch a dream die before your eyes,
And feel it inside and try not to cry.
Then you may strive to ask yourself why
We're all just so desperate to just stay alive?

LOVE AND EARNED SELF-LOATHING

"Love many things, for therein lies the true strength,

and whosoever loves much performs much,

and can accomplish much,

and what is done in love is done well."

- Vincent Van Gogh

HELLO MR. MAGPIE

"Hello Mr. Magpie, and how are you today?"
I say to them in tribute in a funny kind of way.
In those times of language, laughter and smoke,
I told you my feelings in the guise of a joke.
Six weeks 'til September,
not one day spared from thoughts of you,
But you're far too good for me,
and I don't want to look a fool.

This short story had its tragic ending last year,
When all became clear on my first time to hear,
About the only one who stole my breath when first seen,
And how the idealised love was returned upon me.
Autumn turns to ashes
and then I see what you mean,
All the other things made sense
but were failed to be seen.

So now I walk around lamp posts to avoid losing friends,
Mimic your superstitions
so it's like you're around me again.
I love your love of poetry, of partying, dreams and play,
I listened to that song you showed me on repeat for days.
I wish that I'd been braver and tried for what was right,
But all that time convinced myself
that I'm not worth the fight.

I'd like a few new memories;
the ones missed fill me with shame,
First legal drink on me
to make you remember may have been inane.
It may have been futile,
but everyone I meet soon knows your name,
I know I'm two years too late,
but I still think and feel the same.

I swore in ignorance and stubbornness
that it was better not to tell,
But there's nothing left to lose now,
so now I think I might as well.

FOR YOU

If she was born for you, then she was doomed to lose,
Because you don't love her too, whatever she might do.
The beats of her heart speak in code of your name,
Embarrassed by dreams and hiding infinite shame.

In awe of your essence, rendered stumbling and mute,
Blood boiling and rushing to drown denials at the root.
Placed here by fate to carry you through,
She'd lie, cry, or die if it meant she saved you.

Wishing away all your struggles and tears,
She dedicates her soul to you beyond distance and years.
Burning down towers and telling lies to stay true,
Subverting long held ethics with a smile just for you.

She knows how you're different
and understands your resistance,
So she won't interfere
and she'll keep her love at a distance.

She'll be all that you need
without keeping note of the score,
Because she's only for you,
but she deserves so much more.

GOODBYE TEARS

Total strangers meet one day
And both are far from home.
Love at first sight it may not be,
But young hearts tend to roam.
A kiss between them quickly shared
But nothing more can happen here,
They live so far apart that they
Must kiss through goodbye tears.
Young love is sweet and underrated,
Intense and strong and fast,
But unfortunately, like all good things
This love was never meant to last.

OVER MYSELF

It may be hard to believe
that you made such an impression,
But in the brief time I knew you,
my heart learned its lesson.
Mute in admittance, hiding,
downtrodden and reeling,
My lifelong regret will be
that I imprisoned my feelings.

You may claim to be human
like everyone else,
But you are immortal in my heart,
loved over myself.
The second I saw you,
I knew I had to get to know you,
And knowing just fed my longing,
as I suspected that it might do.

It seems common sense to me
that by knowing you any better,
Anyone would love you,
but I just wrote some secret letters:
I had no courage to send them,
for I was convinced I was weak,
So I dared not admit,
though I was always tempted to speak.

Boiling over beneath the surface,
yet self-hating dictated
That I kept my silence from you
and for no good reason, I waited.
I wish I had not,
for now we all know that it's too late,
How could you forgive a spineless coward
and lowlife reprobate?

I grieve for the life
that I missed out on with you
And self-forgiveness escapes me,
for I remained such a fool.
You may reject claims of divinity,
and though that is fine,
I think you are divine
and I still wish you were mine.

While I can admit to
years spent naively idealising,
It may remain to be real,
and I'd relish realising.
I can only promise to be devoted,
and I hope in your heart you can find
The will to grant me a chance
now that I'm more sound of mind.

Of my every desire
you were always the object,
So would you grant me a chance
now that I'm less of a project?
I fear for the answer,
as I know it's too late,
But I have to ask in vain,
as I am cleaning my slate.

And in starting from scratch,
I want to right wrongs I wrought,
By taking the actions which, always,
I explored only in thought.
The curve of your neck
and the motion of your laughter,
Have haunted my dreams,
and will continue hereon after.

I thought I could forget you,
but still I stand in correction,
Remembering a beautiful smile,
on a face of pure perfection.

GHOSTS OF FLOWERS

I wrap myself up in a blanket of denials,
Deny the way I feel for fear of useless trials.
I speak of you in opposites to disguise the way I feel,
All the while longing for precious seconds I could steal.

All this time the time wasn't right,
for one of us, then the other.
And all the while mistaken for just a friend,
a lover or your brother.

Perhaps star-crossed souls
and perhaps something futile,
Ghosts of flowers in fields of lies;
speculation and denial.

Chalice of fire that lights my secret dark heart,
Be inflamed now as the timeless clock mourns.
I present ghosts of flowers in a waking dream
To she who wakes me as she steps into the dawn.

A NOTE TO MY FIANCÉE

You make me feel beautiful in spite of my scars;
Light my inner darkness with your sky full of stars.
You take my disease and make me feel healed,
Where once I was numb, you have allowed me to feel.

You injected such love into a grave full of hate,
Causing what had laid dead for years to reanimate.
Now I try to be a better man, for myself and for you,
Because you deserve only goodness, in life and in truth.

You bring me to life,
though I'm shy and reserved.
And I will try to provide,
all the things you deserve.

Our laughter, our passions,
and our tears all in sync.
You stopped me from falling,
when I was perched on the brink.

You broke through my chains,
and from my prison I'm freed.
You resuscitate my soul,
and are everything I need.

You have given me love,
and all I need for my life.
And I am privileged and honoured
that you'll soon be my wife.

AT MY HANDS

My clumsy, clueless, concrete hands
Have broken things and fractured people.

My stumbling, mumbling, crumbling tongue
Has shattered fragile, invisible bones.

Strangers bare scars from the acid in my throat,
And I will not seek forgiveness until it is deserved.

Shame on me for my past ignorance.
Shame on me for turning sadness into pain.

Shame on yesterday.
Shame on just now.

The salt of your tears still burn the open wounds we share,
With no reprieve for the upturned years and lost steps.

My mistakes are medals pinned directly onto my skin,
Painful adornments,
To commemorate the killings at my hands.

REMEMBER ME

I hope that you remember me as better than I've been,
As the person that I'd like to be,
Not the reality you've seen.
As all the things I want to be and the sacrifices made,
Not just mistakes and weaknesses,
Or the prices we both paid.

I hope that you remember me with tenderness and pride,
Not for the times I failed you, even though I really tried.
As a person who was mostly good,
Even though you saw the bad,
And worked hard on being good enough,
To stop you feeling sad.

I hope that you remember me
With more smiles than I have worn,
And that I bring you happy memories,
Even if you want to mourn.
And I hope you don't forget the times
I put your needs above my own.

And I hope you know my love lives on,
So you'll never be alone.

BREAKING WAVES

Breaking waves of innocence,
By accident, but broken still.
Like the promises of yesteryear,
While we all drank and ate our fill.

Apologies for my own instincts,
For the longing of my past,
For building up hopes in memories
That were not built strong enough to last.

Foundations of good intentions
Prove not fast enough to hold,
But think not they were ever falsehoods;
Only truths were ever told.

But like the setting sun may fall
And light still breaks through the curtain,
It seems the day may be at its end,
But still, we can't be certain.

This sun may still rise another day
And though my will is beckoned,
My head and heart in conflicting roles
Ensure that I'm haunted every second.

So do not take my failings
As any failure on your part
And fear not that any words spoken
Had not come from my heart.

THE BURDEN OF ATLAS

Shoulder the burden of Atlas in my name,
Absorb my failings without question or shame,
Wishing not for a hand that was dealt to elsewhere,
Nor quashing passions or actions;
Always balanced and fair.

You should flee through the night, but here you remain,
Taming dragons of rage and raising a love that lay slain,
Resurrection of loathing builds walls from old stones,
Yet you smash the foundations,
And my sins are atoned.

Begin at the end, and having worked most of the way back,
You built a new city from rubble and still remain on attack.
Blackened heart reanimated,
By the purest innocent in the fight,
Where darkness always follows,
You remained my constant light.

Hope of the hopeless,
My personal saviour has arrived;
Though my inadequacies had killed me,
You make me feel alive.

OF KNOWING OTHER PEOPLE

"Solitude is a chosen separation for not trusting people,
for they dispirit you everytime you try to trust them.
Whereas Isolation is, when you have too many things
to talk about but there's no one for you there."

- *Neymat Khan*

WHAT I HAD NOT KNOWN

I remember the night
A long time ago
When I gave up to you
What I had not known

I gave me in part
A part of my soul
You took out my heart
And took all control

That day brought me tears
When sweet became sour
I could never be right
You kept all of the power

My mouth was dry, my hands were wet
My head was drunk and fate was met
Lost in the plans of what we would get
Scared of the sorrow we know from regret

Forget the whole night
From the time we've outgrown
When I gave up to you
What I had not known

Not warned to be alert
To false kindnesses shown
Worth less than dirt
But I had not known.

WHEN WE NEED TO BLEED

There is undeniable beauty in the brutality of honesty,
but some of my pain remains locked away and unspoken,

because immortalising you in my ink would betray me
worse than you did.

Words can be beautiful catharsis when we need to bleed,
but don't want to cut.

I name my scars after you,
then I pull down my sleeves to cover all traces of you.

I will not grant you the audience you want.

I have denied you like Saint Peter,
and the cockerell has crowed for the both of us.

LONG OF NOTHING

Lives spent in repetition but no-one really cares,
Sit around sharing stories, while spending time to spare.
Feelings shared and blended, love what once was hated,
Begin to renounce feelings and sentiments once stated.
Experience of nothing never felt as good as this,
And the aroma of the feeling is bittersweet and bliss.
Laugh now at tidbits and at how words on their own,
Lacking context, sound ridiculous,
and funny when we're stoned.

Hills just get greener and the sky is more blue,
Life is so funny when I'm here with you.
Lie down in the fields and laugh out loud and away,
Talking long of nothing
as we escape from the day.
Wonder why conflict in time was not lost?
Peace for the earth, and how little the cost?
Expand your mind: you will know this is right,
Love the whole world and resolve not to fight.

But naive as this is and how much it makes sense,
We know this is fleeting and largely pretense.
Mankind is not ready (and too little evolved)
To find their own reason, or truth, or resolve.
Fantasy is futile and it is all that this can breed,
Though we imagine in dreams,
that the like-minded could lead.
We know this is unreachable and is lost in the mire,
Of the pollution of lies and the smoke from their fire.

So we lie down in fields, laughing out loud and away,
Talking long of nothing and living only for today.

A BETTER FRIEND
(FOR C.H.)

I have a very special friend,
Who I will love until life's end,
A friend who's caring, good and kind,
A better friend I cannot find.

Supporting each other through the good and the bad.
I smile at the memories of good times we've had.
We missed the concert, but saved the day,
By going to toy shops to browse and to play.

Cinema trips and our hikes in the hills,
Parties and pubs, drinks and stomachs refilled,
But none are as full as the gratitude I feel,
That you gift me your time and keep your words real.

I value your friendship, for the smiles, laughs and more.
You're my cherished friend who I adore.

THANK YOU FOR HAVING ME

Spinning disc of flashing light
Another troubled beer-soaked night
Swinging a t-shirt over my head
Falling asleep on a makeshift bed
'Broadened' minds discuss at length
If intoxication allows such breadth
Gratefully receiving all you give my way
My way is different and I can't say it pays
Intoxicated strokes of misplaced genius
Created by us, just by drunkenly being us
Often I'm left feeling left far behind
Though it could be me who's ahead sometimes
Coming first in the stagger and the slur of my drawl
But thank you for having me, one friend and all.

BURNING MEMORY LANE

We all know of a place,
Where the sun still shines,
We will all go to the place,
That we keep inside our minds.
The place that cannot be traced,
It exists outside of time.
In the hills of home sweet home
A favourite place of mine.

Memory lane is burning down,
Happy times forgotten now,
Forget this godforsaken town,
Burning down right to the ground.

Looking around in the place that I love,
Admiring the hills and the blue sky above,
Heaven my home, As I stand in the fields,
I wonder if I'm dreaming, This seems so unreal.
Picturesque in every sense,
The fields that flow beyond my fence.
Behind my house and all around,
I'll miss my homely little town.

Memory lane is burning down,
Forgotten times are happier now,
Forget this godforsaken town,
And burn it down, right to the ground.

PAINT MY TURMOIL

Paint my turmoil with your words;
Not one misunderstanding.
Beautiful rendition of ugliness;
Which I could never capture.
Locked inside myself with fear
And it's here that I'll remain,
Freed by your flights of fancy,
Your voice loosens my restraints.

Excuse me while I continue to palpitate.
"How does it feel to be a reprobate?"
Infinity locked inside a figure of eight,
Hate to wait to understand your fate.

Borrow my emotions for your gain,
But not meant to be cruel.
Portray me in ways that I fail to see,
For I am a stranger to myself.
Neither jealous nor angry, but rather in awe;
I accept my place.
Fate is shaped by conditions we choose,
Now you are charged to state my case.

WASTING MY TIME

When you're destroyed and your heart is broke,
You seek solace in company, in drink and in smoke.
Obliterate memory, so the worries just fade,
To the comfort of rain or protection of shade.
No excuses from them, because they just pretend
That they had love for us, yet not even a friend.
So I sit at my keyboard writing a song,
About how once we felt right,
Then they made us feel wrong.
Life was a party, and we had fun for a while,
Forgetting our worries behind harlequin smiles.
Whatever the weather, be it cloudy or fine,
You too can wear smiles while you enjoy wasting time.
Music tastes better and we talk about crap,
That distracts us with laughter to escape from our trap.
So waste time with me and the clouds will not frown,
It's a healthy escape as the smoke filters down.

SLEEP NOW IN PEACE
(FOR LAUREL)

Sleep now in peace
And let all the hurt fall away,
Forever's tragic loss
that you could not stand to stay.
Find strength where you are
And alight your new stage,
Shine as bright in your night
As you had deserved for your day.

THE LOST AND THE MISSED

Falling from grace with eternal thanks,
To rise up again and rebuild hand over fist,
Waiting for changes to shape my self,
In an image of the lost and the missed.

Asking my questions and confessing my ills,
Interpersonal and distant by artful design,
Compliment my mind with my heartsong,
While I find the resolve to claim what is mine.

Whirlpools of confusion have lost me,
I have prayed to beings that do not exist,
The past has coloured my present in crimson
And I long for tidings from the lost and the missed.

CYCLE OF YOU

Shadows of yesterday
Will fall again tomorrow,
Because you shaped a part of everyone you met.
Influence outstanding and heart without question,
The party-time philosopher,
Who partied 'til he slept.

The future selves we spoke of are present in my mind.
Come back for just one day,
So that I can say goodbyes.
I'm in a cycle of you, thinking each time after next,
This agony is meant to fade,
As the years take their effect.

But I'm still reeling from when you left me here alone
And still have your name
And your old number in my phone.
I would have called you sooner, if only I had known,
To laugh and share together;
Growing close and getting stoned.

And I'll tell you how much,
You have always meant to me.
I don't know what I'd say, but I'd try to make you see.
So little was captured from our vast array of memories
But I try to live my life,
As though you're watching over me.

THE EVIL OF THE MIND

"If you know someone who's depressed, please resolve never to ask them why. Depression isn't a straightforward response to a bad situation; depression just is, like the weather. Try to understand the blackness, lethargy, hopelessness, and loneliness they're going through. Be there for them when they come through the other side. It's hard to be a friend to someone who's depressed, but it is one of the kindest, noblest, and best things you will ever do."

- Stephen Fry

DEMONS WILL COME

Demons will come and angels may fade,
Plans are cancelled and new ones are made.
Changes are sought and battles were fought,
With casting aside of the trinkets we bought.

Fallen idols of naive ideals,
Heroes built from truths are proven unreal,
Fantastic lies have laid the foundations,
For pride befallen through degradations.

Licence to grieve being forgone by hate
Has left me numb and low of late.
I fought through the pain I have borne again,
And long for the smiles from way back when.

Wallow in sorrow and claim the cold throne
Of the negative king with his heart of stone.
God-fearing folk shall inherit the meek,
So strong as I was, my body falls weak.

Still, longing and hope have carried me far,
"And though I laid down in gutters, I look to the stars."
Inspired by icons who exceeded their years,
I amassed myself kingdoms despite my own tears.

I wash prizes in blood to show their uniqueness,
I took pride in my scars,
'Til they showed my true weakness.
Now I am cursed for the parts I have played,
For demons will come and the angels shall fade.

THE SCRATCHING

It started as a scratching
which I could barely hear,
I tried hard to ignore it,
but it grew throughout the years.

The scratching grew to whispers,
but I could not see who spoke,
The sound was like a noose
and as it closed on me, I choked.

It only grew much louder
as I fought to close my ears,
I felt the breath upon my cheek,
filling me with fear.

I fought in fear to block it out,
but the whisper raised its voice,
It wailed and screamed and shouted,
until I had no choice.

By then it was too late
and the creature had me fast,
And now it says it owns me
and my future and my past.

It keeps itself in shadow
and I fear to see its shape,
Attempts have proven futile,
So now I don't try to escape.

I even keep my eyes averted
from the shadow that it casts,
But avoidance doesn't save me
and its hold on me still lasts.

THOUGH I LIVE HERE (AMBIGUOUS)

Ambiguous as this may be,
Please won't you hide the way I feel?
Masks of bruises on my face
Trying to hide my true disgrace

Though I live here,
I feel it's not my home
I long to be back where I belong
Where I was not alone.

Home from home sweet home
I'm here again, this time to stay.
Memory becomes new reality,
But might come back to make us pay.

LIKE VELVET

Feeling like nylon around them,
Wishing to feel like velvet again.
Lessons of life are learned from on high,
Fools gold found among disturbed, angry men.
Trying to reach some form of heaven
When the blurry-eyed world is a dream,
Hold a minute long silence for radicals,
Where no one can hear any screams.

LOOSE CANNON IN A HEAD-SPIN

Emotions poured on paper in buckets of blood;
Loose cannon in a head-spin doing more than he should.
Drown me in those buckets if you're misunderstood,
The loose cannon would do it, if he thought that he could.

A legacy created in abstract anger,
Absence of loved ones laid influence bare,
Driven to achieve while I fracture and grieve,
The loose cannon creates chaos without due care.

What once you kept secret is left wide open to see
Because you cast aside the shield that you once held dear,
Barbed wire emotions left to burn on the sea,
Now that it is you who possesses the fear.

WEARY OF WARFARE

I gave up the fight today and just stayed in bed,
I had no energy left to get out of my head.
I surrendered to sadness and wished life away,
And imagined the world if I died where I lay.

In battling myself, I found that I don't fight fair,
Now I'm weary of warfare and no longer care.
No honour in battle, with one man left behind,
Deafened by cannons with surrender in mind.

No parades and no medals, no hero in the fight,
In a war with yourself there's no wrong and no right.
Tired from the trenches and dodging enemy fire,
I handed over my post and, for today, I'll retire.

I'll stare into the dark and hope sleep eats my stay,
Waiting in spite of myself for the next brighter day.

STONE AND STILLNESS

Fear has cast me in concrete.
A statue amongst trees,
Sentenced to watch them grow.

The greys of my mottled skin betray my tribulations,
For time carves its bedpost notches
In our bodies when we're weak.

I am at home in a tomb of stone and stillness,
Camouflaged and safe from
The predators I fear most.

Waters of change have become my mortal enemy,
For they are all that can wear away
The armour of my skin.

Birds of longing have made their nest
On my outstretched arm.
While brighter coloured sisters
fly farther and farther away.

Cold to the touch,
I have tucked away warmth with my courage.
For the unknown is a master
who made this granite cell my home.

I have become a monument,
admired for my unmoving state.
A stationary warning by which others are moved.

FIGHTING THE NIGHTFALL

Fighting the nightfall with matches
and other such efforts in vain,
Like reproducing nothingness,
Just to share and to sustain.

As much as that sounds sad,
Devoid of empathy and downtrodden,
I glare down from the clock tower hungrily,
To rain judgment on this Sodom.

Out of favour with the gods of choice,
and shut out from death's mythologies,
Cast stones into the lush, green riverbed
To extract belated apologies.

Ringing hollow in the night-time,
Falling on deafened ears,
Too late to make a difference;
Wailing underwater through the years.

The sound of cries were stifled
Beneath the ripples of the deep,
So apologies will fail to climb
Upon a mountain of hate so steep.

INSOMNIAC'S LAMENT

Sleep eludes me, and though I have fought,
I cannot escape what my life has wrought.
Tangled in memory and longing for nought,
So that I may sleep, for in dreams I've sought
Escape from Ifs: What I should or I ought,
Though no lesson nor comfort was ever bought.
Beneath the moon, counting stars it has caught,
I lay awake pondering what I was taught;
Useless when measured in what it has brought,
Yet still I lay buried in a grave of thought.

IN THE DARK
(A SONNET ABOUT DEPRESSION)

I wait in the dark for the days to pass,
For daylight and action have charred my skin.
Left out to rot by my brethren en-masse,
Broken and blistered by those allowed in.
Fearing myself and the things I hold true,
Taunted by shadows of misspoken words,
But mostly in fear of things I can't do;
Victories lost to mistakes I preferred.
Drowning in emptiness, choking on fear,
Swaddled in failure and left to lament,
Each tick of a clock counts down a whole year,
Of missteps taken and moments misspent.
Breathing and daylight are lost to my past,
So I hide in the dark; shielded at last.

LOVE AND GUILT
ARE THE BEST OF FRIENDS

Love and guilt are the best of friends, even when they fight.

They go hand in hand against the world,
but turn on each other in an instant, bringing up
painful memories and throwing hateful insults.
Love seems to need guilt around,
to remind us to be grateful and to always try harder.
Guilt tries to push love away,
but then pulls it back in closely, afraid to let go and
hating itself for its own cruelty.

Love and guilt have a toxic, co-dependent relationship,
but they truly believe that they need each other.

Love itself brings guilt into being, to show us every word,
action or thought which betrays us.
Every time we fall short of the expectations we constructed
from the abstract image of what someone else taught us
love is supposed to look like. Guilt arrives soon after.
Guilt feeds on love, because without some level of feeling
and compassion, guilt starves and wastes away to nothing.

Love and guilt would follow each other
to the ends of the earth, and scorch the land as they go.

Even when love is feeling strong
and vibrant and unstoppable, guilt will show up,
unannounced and uninvited.
It brings mistakes or misspoken words,
or sometimes omissions,
which can be just as bad or worse.
The things we have done and the things we forgot to do,
usually presented in bottles
which reek of stale alcohol and poor judgment.

Love and guilt confuse and contradict each other,
but they like it that way.

Guilt is critical of everything.
It tells you to act better, speak better,
love better and feel better.
It tells you when you should have done more,
said more, given more or been more.
Meanwhile, love tells us in a soothing voice that none of
these things are real and that love itself is enough.
But then it invites guilt back in, time and time again,
with open arms, telling us that
things will be better this time.

Love and guilt are the best of friends,
but when they are together, they are no friends of mine.

MOVING UP

Moving up and onward
  In the darkness of the night,
    We did not see the wire,
      We did not have a light.
        Wire across the face
          Can be dangerous indeed,
            But even through the blood-flow,
              You sought to take the lead.

Fate has made us brothers,
  And we'll fight until the end,
    No man will be abandoned,
      For we carry fallen friends.
        Injuries be damned to Hell,
          For we still have steps to take,
            You ignored potential blindness
              On this mission for my sake.

Onwards and upwards
  In the oily black of night,
    Scaling unknown places,
      Unsure which way was right.
        High up on the hilltop,
          Release becomes our goal,
            So we scream into the darkness
              To unleash our tortured souls.

Primal therapy is freeing,
  And we're relieved in primal ways,
    Screaming at the night-time
      Of teenage-angst filled days.
        The streetlights blink below us
          As we scream that youth was killed,
            While the ignorant town lies sleeping
              At the bottom of the hill.

QUENCH

It's hard to explain what causes these moods;
Sometimes hunger for anything other than food,
Or the constant racing without ever coming first,
Or the turbulent rivers which don't quench my thirst.

Smoke rings have failed to impress me of late:
Concealed by mists and the fogs of lost fate.
I disguise myself from loathing, lost now in art,
Disappearing in hiding to restart my heart.

Saltwater rivers battle saltwater tears
And flow into wounds which have not healed for years,
Stinging but healing and cleaning old pains,
Wash away hurt and then we'll see what remains.

Nothing to drink and no food that can fill us,
Our empty insides will be the thing that will kill us.
No winning in running as we stumble downstream,
Constantly tripping on my past and my dreams.

Smoke leaves us blind as the race burns our lungs,
We are cursed to climb ladders without any rungs,
But we still run like the water, in trickles and slow,
On a quest to be nourished by things we can't know.

UNDONE

Unwinding and unravelling
have left me undone.
Broken like the silence
in the chamber of a gun,
Untied and unfinished,
untold lies come unspun,
Exhausted and defeated
with the race still not won.

I have outlived all of my heroes
if you only count the years,
Yet spent my time in shadows,
embracing apathy and fear.
I awaited inspiration
instead of forcing it to appear.
Waiting for the better times,
while neglecting now and here.

Still, I learn lessons
from the things that I destroyed,
Trying to fix habits
to appease those I had annoyed.
Cause less offence through ignorance,
by pouring knowledge into void,
Reclaiming years lost to misery,
which should have been enjoyed.

FRIENDS ARE CRUEL ENDINGS

"Every man has his secret sorrows which the world
knows not; and often times we call a man
cold when he is only sad."
- Henry Wadsworth Longfellow

EGO MASSAGER

Visions in your mind of things that you have seen,
So you tell us all about them,
Then tell us where you've been.
You tell us your life story, though ours don't interest you,
Waiting for strangers' approval,
A pretentious "Yes, me too!"

They all agree with nothing,
While you revel in their praise.
And you reach for inspiration in your lifeless, lost malaise.
Mixed metaphors and similes paired,
From the boring things at hand;
If what you create is artistic, then art itself is damned.

They might appreciate your output,
But do not share your course,
You ignore the struggles of others,
But want sympathy for yours.
Massage your failing ego,
with your fledgling talents on display,
Pollute the world with your production-line,
creating vacuums every day.

MY PUBLIC APOLOGY

Intoxicated and provoked, I spilled out,
Rendering anger in word-clay on illuminated screen.
Emblazoned in hatred, spitting at the contrived,
Grated nerves twisted into accusations and lies.
Recreating insults from diction, I cannot pretend,
Even flowing rivers whisper quiet greatness,
Truly now, I have forged injustice in the end.

Now I doubt too much, they say, and share too much as well.
On the road I walk this is the way, to stick to what you know,
Though between the lines, exposure lurks, shrouded in the dark,
Housed in shallow trenches, soaked in petrol, near a spark.
If that's the way I see it, then that's what I will say.
Not for the best, because it can cause some offence,
Great apologies to you, but it wasn't for you anyway.

THE REMAINS

Enveloped in darkness, now I'm blinded by trust,
I find myself betrayed and have been left out to rust.
Like a broken-down tractor carcass rotting in the field,
Abandoned to die, but to decay is to yield.

So I fight against nature to revive all that flowers,
Dividing my soul to rain down good will in showers.
But opposition of nature and my own freedom curtailing,
Have yet been in vain and produced nothing but failings.

The farmhouse, abandoned, stands alone and neglected,
Bones remain of the animals and crops wither, infected.
Autumn is welcome as it signals the beginning of our end,
No longer longing for better and no more need to pretend.

Used and abused at the changing whims of my lessers,
They have littered my mind with a cacophony of stressors.
Leaves on the wind shall carry my tributes through ages;
Death in nature pours no mourning onto,
Yellow, saddened pages.

Poison ivy forms the net behind which I hide myself away,
I'll lay still enough for moss to hide the signs of my decay.
And though I tried in vain,
To outgrow these natural chains,
I became a feast for vultures who grew fat on my remains.

KINGS OF EXCUSES

Numbness is welcome until it's all that you feel,
Then emotions are milestones which make the blur real.
We stay blind to the self, and all our wants melt away
We long for the abuses that we endured yesterday.

We hear the kings of excuses,
And the selfish things they do,
With pride in their hate and in their drive to be cruel.
Teasing out rage like red rags waved to bulls,
They pull things from our brains,
And take root in our skulls.

Old ideals lost without planning or patent,
All dolls and toys to be played with by Satan.
Incubate thoughts, because we hate us the most,
But we'll burn down their lives, not leaving one ghost.

CRUCIFICTION OF THE FAITHFUL

Dip me in ink, for I have martyred the sword:
Broken by design, or so I'd pretend to afford.
Louder than the death of a lonely, silent fiction,
Imprisoned by limitations of some extensive diction.

Tell stories filled with monsters,
And demons, borne from Hell,
Answer the call when you hear the tolling of the bell.
So remind me of laughter if you can remember it yourself,
I will not laugh along with you,
In the sake of laughter for itself.

Write me off as a failure and I'll be strangely grateful,
Betray me fairly often and yet always I'll stay faithful.
Memories are fleeting and I have found that even more,
I forget to remember that your riches left me poor.

I have an aptitude for failing and for falling from up high,
Born in itself from naive trusting of your lies.
But strength is found in numbers,
And your value dwindles still,
I'll starve myself so I can purge,
Upon your soul to gain my fill.

Monsters come at night-time and hide beneath your bed,
But the demons of my memories,
Are those you planted in my head.
Yet crucified am I, for the way I have been created,
Punished by and for the sins that others perpetrated.

DEAD AND GONE

I've told the story once before
Of a boy who only wanted more
Now he's dead and gone for good
This boy never did do what he could

There was once a girl who could achieve
But before she could, she had to leave
A boy thought she deserved a throne
This boy she left here all alone

His failures grew and brought more stress
He failed to find that one success
He failed in love and happiness
He failed to see how he was blessed

The boy was left alone and scared
He could not turn to anywhere
His family were all dead and gone
He had no friend except this one

The boy had dreams of happiness
But they were cast aside for less
He wanted purpose and a bit of pride
And to leave a legacy before he died

His failures grew and brought more stress
He failed to find that one success
He failed in love and happiness
He failed to see how he was blessed

So, after years of torturous life
He found some luck and found a wife
But she betrayed his trust and then
He tumbled down from grace again

This was all too much for him
He wanted to just give it in
He wished that he would fall down dead
He put a gun against his head

His failures grew in heartbreak and stress
He failed to find that one success
He failed in love and happiness
He failed to see how he was blessed

Now the boy is dead and gone
His dreams undone, but life goes on
Saddest of all, as he knew all along,
He was never missed by anyone

RETREAT

Open up your feelings
When you want or need to shout,
Pry the lock on Pandora's box
And let all the demons out.

The day before I died again
I looked back on life and cried
For each and every speck of time;
I had wasted all of mine.

No more civil niceties,
No more heartfelt words,
No more bowing down in servitude,
Now it's my time to be heard.

My lifeblood runs much colder,
My heavy heart has drowned,
I submit to feeling older
But still search for my hometown.

Mercy is for the weak of pocket,
And you might brand me a freak,
But light cannot shine upon itself,
Yet it forces darkness to retreat.

I illuminate your shadows
And you do the same for me,
Fearless in your criticism,
And toxic in your speech.

So, open up your feelings
When you want or need to shout,
Pry the lock on Pandora's box
And let all the demons out.

THE MISSING HOPES I FOUND

Longing to seek what I was always scared to find,
Looking to the light that will inevitably leave me blind.
Illusions wrapped in fantasy are lies to my own mind:
Delusions to deceive me that I need another kind.

Shunning what I know to be the best for my well-being,
What needs to be contained,
Confused with things we should be freeing.
Running from yourself and me,
Towards everything I've been fleeing,
Blinded by the light of truth,
Which I'm still too far from seeing.

Surprising to myself and yet, it is your forté to astound,
Lost and lonely in the oceans
Of the missing hopes I found,
Palpitating hearts drown out the storm
With penetrating sound,
And there is no escape in sleep,
Nor in seeking solid ground.

When I rise, I'll drown myself in the vast expanse of waves,
Giving in to certainty and to the unknown things I crave.
Deafened by the silence that I can hear amongst the graves,
My fallen wanting waiting for the light I aim to save.

DROWN

I had thought that with you, I was understood,
But now I shall drown, like you said that I should.
Cast aside crutches to prove a moot point,
And I'll suffer in silence for your soul to anoint.

My failings are many, I shall never deny,
So no need to embellish, imagine or lie.
Rejection of apologies can splinter the heart,
And here I lay shattered, in heartbroken parts.

I was already broken and I thought you agreed
That destruction is distraction and can be what I need.
Regardless, I'll prove that your fears are unfounded.
Even at my own detriment, I'll keep myself grounded.

Though my progress will be stunted in repairing my soul,
I will still prove the point before I make myself whole.
While here I lay rotting, crying always inside,
Do not ask what I'm thinking, for now I must hide.

From myself, my emotions, memory and strife,
Unforgiven, though innocent: Punished by life.
The darkness inside does not feel fear from the light
But has swallowed it whole in an expression of might.

I will wait for distraction,
To soothe the wounds of my heart,
But for now I'll keep drowning
Until the healing can start.

MISTAKEN

I may have been mistaken, so correct me if I'm wrong,
But I thought I was a friend to you,
When you didn't feel so strong?
And I remember being there for you,
When you had barely anyone else.
Providing a shoulder to cry on,
About how being different felt.
And I don't make good friends easily,
So it was hard to let you close,
Which is why my own naivety,
Might be the part that stings the most.
In search of our identities and exploring
Who we were and are, secure in mutual company,
Sharing and caring under Manchester stars.

But I clearly was mistaken,
For betrayal came without a pause,
And I doubt you're even sorry,
For the insecurities you've caused.
So pardon me if I don't forgive,
And I know I'll never forget.
I'm still hesitant to trust,
Because of the burns from your regrets.
You're one of the main reasons,
That I always keep my circles small;
You taught me that longevity is no gauge of trust at all,
And growing up with someone,
In proximity and in deeds,
Is no guarantee of loyalty,
If they have slight reasons to deceive.

So I'm sorry that I was mistaken
In my assumption that we were friends,
And I'm sorry you think I'm unreasonable
For not forgiving you in the end.
You ripped out my heart without the slightest hint of guilt,
For the sake of cheap orgasms
At the expense of everything I'd built.
And even now you're thinking,
That it's on me to move on and forgive,
Convinced out of necessity,
That victims should live and let live.
But ethics do not care for age;
Not excused by the years that passed,
I have known better all along,
Fifteen years ago or the day before last.

You taught me friends are cruel endings,
Waiting for their appointment.
So now I'm a social minimist,
To minimise my disappointments,
And now you think I'm unreasonable,
For holding a grudge for so long.
But can you blame a bird with scars in its throat,
If it offered you no song?
And I know I've been mistaken,
But I was corrected by your wrong,
You have been no friend to me,
And you stopped me feeling strong.

CLOUDS OF ABSENCE

Through deep, insightful tomes,
And pages I have thumbed,
But grief, as always, has left me,
Sedated and so numbed.
Tales of redemptions,
Rendered meaningless by a hollowed soul;
Loss is not to have never gained,
But to forgo any and all control.

Fall foul of immortals in thoughts,
Plans and then in deeds,
As the attraction of this indulgence,
Is in its power to impede.
I simply crave to be numb,
For I am exhausted from a life of pain.
And shame from blame-games,
In the name of those who share the same.

So now shield me in memory,
For the present moment is pure hell.
Overshadowing the depths,
Of the narratives we wish to tell.
To forget is an injustice,
And to ignore is tantamount to sin;
Sharing only in fractions or segments,
Is inviting pain to dwell within.

Tributes are obscured,
In clouds of absence and in pools of tears,
So indulge in the lessons learned and reject related fears.
With malice aforethought,
And responding justly and in kind,
We try not to forget,
That it is your memory on our minds.

Contradictory and difficult,
In equal measures to your redemptions,
Teaching fitting lessons to us by virtue of stark exemptions.
Weather the harsh and unfair,
For none of us are innocent of that.
You and I learned from experience,
And were truly grateful for the fact.

'If minds were universal…'
And other wishful thoughts
Would dissipate this conflict,
Forcing action as it ought.
But dreams are for the weak and hearts will always fight
When no one side is wrong,
Nor is the other side quite right.

Meaning no harm,
Nor to commit some heinous crime,
Please forgive conflicts of interest,
That may sour this time.
Fear not that this story is all of you that I will tell,
This is simply my apology,
And I still owe you my farewell.

HABIT OF FORGIVENESS

For once I feel sickened by you, who I love,
And I can feel the sickness inside me, growing.
Have you ever felt the poison of your own tongue?
Have you ever struck out at yourself without knowing?

Why would you choose to say those harsh words,
While omitting the part that you know I'd want to hear?
Am I just sickened at the words that you said to me,
Or am I more so by the fact that they fill me with fear?

This is the second time this has happened
And, in faith, I forgave you the first,
But I'm in the habit of forgiveness now
And no longer surprised when I get hurt.

I had thought you had felt the same way as me
When I said that I love you like no others.
You have always been more than just 'there' for me;
We shared a bond as strong as brothers.

Now this sickness is holding me strong,
I fear I cannot view you the same way again.
Most would have considered a friend's feelings first,
Now what if I can never see you the same?

But then, I'm in the habit of forgiveness now,
So that's one more hurt that I'll just have to allow.

TOUCHED

You touched my soul with acid hands,
Changing me forever in a painful instant
That I never want to take back.
Forgetting is a dream I hesitate to conjure.

Your fingers slipped around my heart so delicately,
You didn't even break my skin,
But you balled up your fists and pulled away,
Splintering my ribs into the dust of a crumbling sky.

I have screamed you from my blackened lungs,
And bled you from narrowing veins,
I have cried you from my tired eyes,
But I cannot beat you out of my drowning heart.

My entry wounds resemble your teeth marks,
From where you ate the parts you considered best,
Leaving exit wounds in the shape
Of your razor-wire influence.
Scarring me just enough,
To remind me never to trespass again.

Time renders all of us mute,
With swollen tongue and desert mouth.
But solace can be found in knowing
That it does the same to grief.

REACHING EVER UPWARDS

"There are far, far better things ahead
than anything we leave behind."

- *C.S. Lewis*

PURGATORY'S PRISONER

Perpetual blur of a still horizon
With silent slow-moving parts,
Locked in low gear and cursed to keep creeping;
A stutter of hopeful false starts.

Purgatory's prisoner survives only on will;
On hope against hope in the dark.
With fingers outstretched, which was always in vain,
But through the clouds there appears a small spark.

The flash in the night feeds the will to keep fighting
Against invisible shackles and binds.
A glimpse of the Hell in this solitary cell
Is just a taster of sight to the blind.

Enough to assess and to form a prognosis
For standing back up when we fall,
The impetus needed to set into motion
A climb beyond self-imposed walls.

Standing on atrophied limbs for the first time
In an age of endless nights without day,
Yet here comes the morning with promise of changes,
Caressing this prison in the sun's loving rays.

IN THE PIT OF A WELL

In the pit of a well was darkness
and in that dark there dwelled a soul,
Lost to time most infinite,
bereft of hopes and dreams and goals.
But from the depths there grew a ladder,
made entirely of weeds;
Nature's rejects in conspiracy
to ensure the soul be freed.

Though fearful of the light
and of the unknown beyond the walls,
The soul ascended skyward,
thus reversing its past falls.
The climb was slow and painful,
for the ladder bore great length
And the soul had long lay silent
without calling on its strength.

Adrenaline is only human,
so the soul lacked such benefits,
But the task at hand promised freedom;
escape from the dark infernal pit.
The soul called on strength eternal,
though knew not from whence it came
And emerged into the sunlight,
free of shackles, fear and shame.

But once out, the soul heard calling
from deep within the well,
Beckoning it back again
to be cocooned in shadows' shell.
Battling the temptation
of the safety in familiar binds,
The soul walked away with confidence
of the happiness it shall find.

EVERY DAY

Every day is a reminder of how short life can be,
So fill yours with laughter and rejoice that you're free.
Look inside yourself and there you shall seek,
Your own cure for loneliness while remaining unique.

The evening of life approaches, the sunset growing near,
But the answers live inside you and there is nothing to fear.
Morning is new life, with promises of sights unseen,
To do whatever we choose to do; to live and love and
dream.

We always think we know that another morning follows,
But no-one truly knows what's held inside tomorrow.
Live for the moment we are always told,
Treat every second as precious as gold.

Speak all your feelings, but then learn to heed;
Never impose and just let others be.
There are those who don't listen to the words that you say,
But belief in ourselves can be a source of great faith.

Remember the promise that you can live evermore,
Just as each day sees dawn and opens more doors.
Love lasts forever; even outlasting death,
As long as you love, you always have something left.

Do not be consumed by possessions and greed;
Materials mean nothing to those who are free.
Family and health are the true sources of pleasure,
To have these and friends is the only true treasure.

Now we wait for tomorrow and the challenges it brings
And we thank life itself for all of these things.

HOPE IS LIKE AN ECHO

Hope is like an echo in a warm, tiny room.

The people sitting in there don't even notice it anymore.

It has always just been there,
Hugging the ends of their sentences,
With comforting agreement.
Acknowledging them, reassuring them,
Muttering repetitions in emphatic resonance.

But to those who are only visitors,
The echo is loud and beautiful. It overpowers. It envelops.

The echo draws them, but they do not fully understand it,
because it has been absent from them.

They try to chase it, to catch it, to touch it and hold it.
But there is no hardness to an echo,
No solid parts to grab it.

It hears someone speak and it comes,
Bowing and dipping as it follows each master.

The visitors don't realise that here, in this new place,
The echo will be there for them too.
All they have to do is make a sound.

It might even happen by accident,
But the echo rewards everyone regardless.
It needs only some small action or a single syllable.

You need not search for the echo,
Because the echo finds you.
It will embrace your words and whisper them back to you,
just as it does for the others.

You just have to do or say something.
Anything. Then the echo will come.

It can not be bottled or packaged to be taken away for later,
Or to give to someone else.

Your echo can only belong to you.
It is in you and it is of you.

The echo follows sound just as hope follows action.

If you make music, then the echo sings back.
If you scream in primal release,
It will briefly take over while you refill your lungs.

It never interrupts, never deviates, never smothers.
It simply reflects what it receives and extends it,
Slightly further forward in time.

It carries our intention onwards.

A certain future, created by our now.

...

Hope is like an echo in a warm, tiny room.

You're welcome to make a sound.

DEATH UNDONE

The snowy mountain tops are melting
in the heat of midday sun,
Though what's ugly beneath is bared to all,
it signals death undone.

Rising from the earth like a seedling sprouting,
reaching to the sky,
Freedom from the grounding of hatred,
and of bitterness and lies.

Bearing fruit of worthwhile labours,
though still awaiting harvest time,
And with bated breath anticipating
some justice to fit the crimes.

Time's healing properties are a gift
that I continue to receive,
The temptation is to thank some gods,
though I still fail to believe.

Hatching from a casing of barbed thorns,
blood and sharpened tongues,
Eyes opening in light for the first time in years
and now here I long to belong.

Falling from a height from which
no thing could hope to survive,
My wings have begun to open
and I believe that I can stay alive.

SEEDLINGS

Neglected seedlings withered
on a dusty windowsill,
Revived by acts of kindness
and growing stronger still.

Quenched by running waters
of a loving hand and care,
Now reaching ever upwards
with grace and strength beyond compare.

Enriched by beams of daylight
and nourished upwards from the roots,
Becoming newly born majestic,
finally bearing rightful fruit.

Grow forth in newfound freedom,
touch sky and birth new seeds,
Be in this light eternal,
for the dark served no good deeds.

THE PERFORMER

I was a child performer,
but not on film or TV screens,
I was a singing, dancing, acting star,
just not one you would have seen.
My stage was family living rooms,
but they were arena shows to me,
No obscure role and no audience
was ever too small to please.
I was a child performer,
in classroom choirs and church-hall plays,
Living for a spotlight
where I could play away my days,
On high school stage and playground fields,
wherever I found roles,
Wherever there were laughs to steal
or stories to be told.
I was blind to ridicule
and to mockery and to sneers,
But you were sure to emphasise
that I'd been wrong for all these years.
You made sure to bring my confidence
right down to match your own,
And I learned that making laughter
made me a fool now that I'm grown.
Only later I saw through it
and realised your poisoned view
Was actually nothing to do with me,
but everything to do with you.

You made me think that laughter
was always meant to be cruel,
But you're not clever enough to be funny,
so in your case it rings true.
So now I'm free of your hatred
for the expressive things I did,
And maybe I'll recapture the spirit
of that performing kid.
I'll feel no shame for performing,
although not as naturally as before,
But I was a child performer
and I'll climb onto the stage once more.
And though my audience is small,
I never wanted to be a star,
Just to be a performer,
in the warm confidence
where spotlights are.

THE SMALLEST FOUNDATIONS

While you look around for purpose,
Your eyes belay an indication
That you dismiss cliches and platitudes
With passive indignation.
But often they become such
because wisdom bears repeating,
In metaphors and allegories:
lessons learned in seconds fleeting.
Weep not for lost hours,
for weeks, months or seasons,
But find your own meaning
and make your own reasons.
Show passion for yourself,
as you would for your distractions,
No dreams are attained by desire alone,
without taking up some action.

The smallest foundations laid
when you cannot build too much,
Begins reconstructing cities
which have lain to waste, untouched.
Rivers may run deep,
with treacherous breadth and length,
But struggles are but stepping stones
upon which we walk to strength.
It may be easier said than done
when the world is painted black,
But take pride in what you have
and not despair for what you lack.
Push the self to shun convention
and not succumb to greed,
Not with half of what we want,
but with everything we need.

AS ONLY YOU CAN

You're unique on the inside with something to give,
A perspective or story to share or relive.
An interest you always thought was quite useless
Might be just the thing to give your life purpose.

A plant cannot grow until somebody seeds it,
So share what you have, because somebody needs it.
Each talent a gift which someone, somewhere will treasure,
Perhaps with a message, or even just to bring pleasure.

There is no cause greater than to entertain or to teach,
Or to move others to achieve
what they believed they can't reach.
All of these bring joy and hope
and build up kindred spirits,
So paint, or sculpt, or write, or sketch,
or sing your homegrown lyrics.

No failure is worse than the crime of not trying,
So share hidden talents which
your fear has been denying.
And bring into the light whatever you've been hiding
Because searching outside you
reveals nothing worth finding.

You are strength, you are hero, you are warrior and art,
You are a sky wrapped around worlds
inside a still-beating heart.
There's been uniqueness within you since this life began,
So breathe life into the world, as only you can.

HAPPY

Depression is lies, yet it rings true in me
So I fight with conviction for happiness' sake,
I know this is trickery, so I argue my case
To release real smiles, even if they seem fake.

The smile I had lost has finally returned,
The dark seems far when surrounded by friends.
Laughter rings out, a sweet hopeful sound,
It's all down to you that I have no fear of the end.

This too shall pass, so reject your mind's lies
Happy is in you, and in the gifts we've been sent,
There can always be hope and some shred of light
It's about what you have, not in what you lament.

ACKNOWLEDGEMENTS

There are a lot of people I want to thank, without whom this collection never would have happened. First of all, thanks to my wife, the most wonderful, caring and patient person I ever met. You deserve better than I can ever give you and I'm lucky to be loved by someone as amazing as you.

Eternal thanks to my parents for always accepting and encouraging me, even at the times (which have probably been many) when I was more of a challenge than a source of pride. My parents always stressed the importance of reading and learning, and introduced me to a wide range of genres. They encouraged my creativity and tried to support me in every way they possibly could. Thank you also to the rest of my family, who have tried their best with me when I have been difficult and have always been supportive of my writing.

To my incredible friends Vincent Heselwood and Martin Redmond (the fantastic bastard), I really can't thank either of you enough for helping me edit this collection. You are both better friends than I deserve. Thank you for your friendship and support throughout the years.

Also to Carl Lord, Chrissy Coleman and the whole Coleman family, as well as the rest of the Heselwood family, who all encouraged and supported me. You all helped me become a better person in one way or another and I thank you from the bottom of my heart.

Next, I want to thank all of the teachers who gave me the opportunity and skills to grow as a writer, who introduced me to the writers who shaped me and who gave me knowledge and support. Your work is vastly underappreciated. I especially want to mention John Pocock, Gill Armour, Paul Howarth and Rod Hall, who all played a large part in inspiring me to pursue writing as a hobby and career.

To the counsellors who have helped me through some of the hardest times in my life and helped to make me a better, stronger, and more authentic person, particularly Helen, Peter, and Adam. These people dedicate their professional lives to helping others and giving people the tools to help themselves. You all helped and encouraged me to believe in myself. Of those three, a special thanks to Adam for giving me the final push to put my work out into the world.

Thank you very much to Ria for being a friend when I needed one, enduring my tears and hard times, encouraging me, and being a constant throughout years of too much change. Also for taking this chaotic mess of words and turning it into an actual book. Thank you for helping me achieve this dream.

To the people who have helped me through hard times, who occasionally showed me the good side of the human race, who saved my life when I was completely lost and who ever showed me any kindness and compassion, I thank you from the pit of my soul. I would not be here without you and I wish you all every success and happiness in life.

Huge thanks to Shaun Hutson, Nicholas Vince, Kealan Patrick Burke, Liian Varus, David Gelmini and J.M. Ritch, who all read a preview of this book and contributed the praise which has been quoted at the front. Thank you so much for taking the time to read my work and for allowing me to use your kind words.

Lastly, massive thanks to the incredibly talented illustrators who contributed to this book, Andy Hosegood and Coral Davies. Your awesome artwork really compliments my words, and I am extremely grateful for the pieces that you have been able to create and contribute.

Thank you all for making this possible.

ABOUT THE AUTHOR

N.P. Hunt is a writer from Greater Manchester, who lives in Oldham with his wife and their beautiful dog, Quinzel. He is a former milkman, factory worker, shoe shop salesman, customer service advisor, self defense consultant and kitchen assistant (none of which he did very well) and currently works as a security guard. After writing poetry and fiction for over twenty-three years, he was encouraged to publish some of his work by a counsellor he was seeing for depression-related issues. This is his first book.

Thank you for reading. If you enjoyed this collection, please show your support by leaving a review on Amazon, Goodreads, or any book review site.

Reviews help authors to be seen by readers and help other readers like yourself find books they'll enjoy. It doesn't have to be detailed and only takes a few moments, but makes a huge difference.

Find out more about N.P. Hunt's work at **www.NPHuntWriter.com**

&*

*In loving memory of six hundred and forty two ampersands, lovingly replaced with the word 'and'. N.P. Hunt loves &. Gone but not forgotten.